Let It Right First Time
A Landlord & Letting Agent Guide

Rob Bryer

Copyright © 2023 Robert Bryer

All rights reserved.

ISBN: 9781546984337

Who am I and why should you listen to me?

I have spent my life in property and finance. Starting at a young age as a trainee financial advisor I went on to set up my own company at 27 years old. After initially starting a mortgage brokerage I quickly set up two high street agencies. Seeing the changing market I set up the first hybrid agency in 2010. This led to having agents right across the country from Cornwall to Aberdeenshire trading under my company "The Good Estate Agent". I am a qualified Letting & Estate Agent, member of ARLA (Association of Residential Letting Agent) & NAEA (National Association of Estate Agents) and CeMap qualified mortgage broker. I have trained over 400 agents, sold and let 1000's of properties and have my own portfolio of property investments.

Between my wife and I there is nothing we don't know about property and finance. My wife, Sue Bryer, is the expert on all things inventory and deposit related and she's written her own book on the subject. We will cover some of this in the book but if you love detail it's well worth a look.

CONTENTS

LEGAL:

THE INFORMATION PROVIDED WITHIN THIS
CONTENT IS FOR GENERAL INFORMATIONAL
PURPOSES ONLY AND IS NOT INTENDED TO
PROVIDE LEGAL OR PROFESSIONAL ADVICE.
WHILE WE STRIVE TO PROVIDE ACCURATE AND
UP-TO-DATE INFORMATION, WE MAKE NO
REPRESENTATIONS OR WARRANTIES OF ANY
KIND, EXPRESS OR IMPLIED, ABOUT THE
COMPLETENESS, ACCURACY, RELIABILITY,
SUITABILITY OR AVAILABILITY WITH RESPECT
TO THE INFORMATION, PRODUCTS, SERVICES,
OR RELATED GRAPHICS CONTAINED IN THIS
CONTENT FOR ANY PURPOSE. ANY RELIANCE
YOU PLACE ON SUCH INFORMATION IS
THEREFORE STRICTLY AT YOUR OWN RISK.

IN NO EVENT WILL WE BE LIABLE FOR ANY
LOSS OR DAMAGE INCLUDING WITHOUT
LIMITATION, INDIRECT OR CONSEQUENTIAL
LOSS OR DAMAGE, OR ANY LOSS OR DAMAGE
WHATSOEVER ARISING FROM LOSS OF DATA OR
PROFITS ARISING OUT OF, OR IN CONNECTION
WITH, THE USE OF THIS CONTENT.

THE INCLUSION OF ANY LINKS OR REFERENCES
TO THIRD-PARTY WEBSITES, PRODUCTS, OR
SERVICES DOES NOT NECESSARILY IMPLY A
RECOMMENDATION OR ENDORSEMENT BY US.
WE HAVE NO CONTROL OVER THE NATURE,
CONTENT, AND AVAILABILITY OF THOSE SITES,
PRODUCTS, OR SERVICES.

1 INTRODUCTION: STARTING YOUR JOURNEY AS A LANDLORD OR LETTING AGENT

Why become a landlord or letting agent?

Every individual's journey into the world of property letting is unique. You may be a first-time landlord seeking guidance, a seasoned landlord looking to enhance your knowledge, or someone who recently acquired a property through purchase or inheritance. Perhaps you're considering a career change and are interested in becoming a letting agent. Regardless of your motivation, this book aims to provide the answers you need to make informed decisions and achieve success in property letting.

The rental property business can be a highly rewarding career path for both landlords and letting agents. However, this success depends on making the right decisions from the outset. Mistakes can lead to considerable headaches, and rectifying them may not be a quick or straightforward process. Therefore, it's crucial to pay attention to every aspect of property letting and avoid rushing into agreements with unsuitable tenants.

As I write this introduction, my wife has just returned from conducting several property inspections. She found the experience gratifying, as each tenant expressed their satisfaction with our services and appreciation for how well they've been treated. One tenant was particularly impressed that a tap issue was resolved within 24 hours. Although we consider such responsiveness standard practice, it's a stark contrast to the experiences of many tenants in the letting industry.

Our business philosophy is simple: treat every customer as you would treat your friends. By looking after your tenants and addressing their concerns promptly, they are more likely to respect you and your property.

Staying involved in your business

Despite managing a large organization with over 100 staff members and franchisees, my wife and I find it essential to maintain a hands-on approach to our business. Staying involved in every aspect of the company allows us to remain in touch with its day-to-day operations. We firmly believe in leading by example and would never ask anyone to do something we wouldn't do ourselves. Whether it's moving furniture, conducting last-minute cleaning, or addressing urgent issues such as blocked toilets, being proactive and responsive is vital to success in the property letting industry. That said, where I can leverage my time I do and my own property portfolio is largely managed by my company, The Good Estate Agent, giving me time to grow my businesses and acquire more property. We have recently picked up keys to a Georgian Farmhouse which we intend to be our family home. With multiple barns and outbuildings the gross development value of this property will be £4 million but the cost to us was virtually nothing. We will be documenting how we did this and our journey on my social media channels so follow me on Instagram @rob.bryer to find out more.

Now that you know a bit about our approach and philosophy, it's time to dive into the book and explore the world of property letting. Here's to your success!

Top Tips:

1. Determine your motivation for becoming a landlord or letting agent. Are you seeking a career change, looking to enhance your knowledge, or have recently inherited a property? Understanding your motivation will help guide your decisions and actions.

2. Pay attention to every aspect of property letting and avoid rushing into agreements with unsuitable tenants. Making the right decisions from the outset is crucial to success.

3. Treat every customer as you would treat your friends. Address tenant concerns promptly and look after your tenants. This will help ensure they respect you and your property.

4. Stay involved in your business and maintain a hands-on approach. Leading by example and being proactive and responsive is vital to success in the property letting industry.

5. Keep an open mind and be willing to learn. The property letting industry is constantly changing, and there is always room to improve your knowledge and skills.

Chapter 2: Prioritising Safety: Regulations and Best Practices

Introduction: The Importance of Safety and Compliance

While discussing health and safety may seem tedious, it is a critical aspect of property management. Ensuring the safety of your tenants and adhering to legal requirements should be your top priority. Failing to do so may result in legal trouble or a heavy burden on your conscience. Fortunately, understanding and implementing the necessary safety measures is relatively straightforward once you know your responsibilities.

Gas Safety

Gas safety is a crucial aspect of property

management. If your property has gas appliances, you must obtain a gas safety certificate from a registered Gas Safe engineer. This inspection should cover every gas appliance, including boilers, hobs, and heaters.

A gas safety certificate is valid for 12 months, and you should ensure it has at least six months remaining at the start of each new tenancy. Failure to comply with gas safety regulations is a criminal offence and can result in severe penalties, including imprisonment. Annual gas safety checks typically cost around £100 per year depending on your area. Establish a system to track when your gas safety certificate expires, and consider working with a reputable letting agent who can remind you when it is due and help arrange the inspection in good time.

Electrical Safety

Since June 2020, new electrical safety regulations require all new tenancies to have a safety certificate, with existing tenancies requiring certification from April 1st, 2021. The cost of an electrical safety certificate is approximately £150, and it is usually valid for five years.

Additionally, consider having your electrical appliances PAT tested annually, which costs around

£10 per appliance.

Smoke and Carbon Monoxide Alarms

It is now a legal requirement for all tenanted properties to have a working smoke alarm on each floor. These alarms should be tested on the move-in day, with the responsibility of testing and changing batteries then shifting to the tenant.

Carbon monoxide detectors are also legally required. Installing and maintaining these devices can help prevent dangerous situations and give you peace of mind.

For certain property types, such as HMOs (houses in multiple occupation), more stringent rules apply. Mains interlinked smoke detectors and heat detectors in kitchens may be required, so always seek professional advice.

Legionella Risk Assessment

The Health and Safety Executive recommends conducting a legionella risk assessment every two years. This assessment ensures water is at the correct temperature and eliminates potential sources of bacterial growth.

Simple measures, such as installing tank lids, flushing empty properties, and addressing dead pipes or leaks, can significantly reduce the risk of legionella. You can conduct this assessment yourself or enlist a professional to help.

Energy Performance Certificates (EPCs)

While not directly related to safety, EPCs are a legal requirement for all advertised rental properties in the UK. These certificates assign an energy rating to the property.
Since April 2018, private rental properties must have a minimum EPC rating of E. Failure to comply can result in penalties of up to £4,000.

Mortgages and Insurance

If your property has a mortgage, inform the lender of your intention to rent. Obtain permission before a tenant moves in, and be prepared to provide a copy of the lease if requested. Some lenders may charge a small administrative fee.

As a landlord, you remain responsible for building insurance, which covers fixtures and fittings but not carpets. If your property is furnished or partially furnished, consider contents insurance.

Tax and Overseas Landlords

Rental income is subject to tax, so consult an

accountant for advice. Landlords residing overseas can apply for an exemption certificate to receive gross rent. If an exemption is not obtained, letting agents or tenants must deduct tax at the lowest prevailing rate and issue a certificate at the end of each tax year.

Council Tax

Most councils charge landlords council tax during vacant periods, regardless of whether the property is furnished or unfurnished. Therefore, minimising void periods is crucial to avoid additional expenses.

Now that we have covered the essential safety and legal aspects of property management, we can move on to presenting your property in the best possible light.

General Maintenance and Repairs

Regularly maintaining your property and promptly addressing any repair needs is essential for the safety and satisfaction of your tenants. By proactively attending to these issues, you can prevent more significant problems and costly repairs down the line.

Schedule routine property inspections to identify and resolve maintenance issues. Keep a record of all repairs and maintenance activities to track expenses and ensure legal compliance.

Asbestos Management

If your property was built before 2000, it may contain asbestos. As a landlord, you are responsible for managing any asbestos-containing materials (ACMs) in the property. The first step is to arrange an asbestos survey to identify any ACMs present.

Upon identifying ACMs, establish an asbestos management plan, outlining how you will manage and monitor the materials to ensure tenant safety. The plan should include regular inspections, proper labelling of ACMs, and providing tenants with information about the presence of asbestos.

Tenant Communication

Establishing clear and open communication with your tenants is essential for maintaining a safe and pleasant living environment. Encourage tenants to report any safety concerns or maintenance issues immediately. Provide multiple contact options, such as email, phone, or an online portal, to facilitate easy communication.

Developing a positive relationship with your tenants can encourage them to respect your property and help create a safe environment for everyone involved.

Accessibility

Ensure your property is accessible to all tenants, including those with disabilities. Evaluate the property for potential accessibility issues, such as narrow doorways, stairs without handrails, or insufficient lighting.

Consider making reasonable adjustments to accommodate tenants with disabilities, such as installing grab bars in the bathroom or adding ramps for wheelchair access. By making your property accessible, you create a safer and more inclusive living environment.

In Conclusion

Safety and legal compliance are critical components of responsible property management. By prioritising tenant safety, adhering to legal requirements, and proactively addressing potential issues, you can create a secure and pleasant living environment for your tenants while minimising potential legal and financial risks.

With the necessary safety and legal considerations in place, you can now focus on presenting your property in its best light to attract high-quality tenants and secure a successful rental experience.

Top tips:

1. Stay on top of gas safety by obtaining a gas safety certificate from a registered Gas Safe engineer. Ensure the certificate has at least six months remaining at the start of each new tenancy and establish a system to track when the certificate expires.

2. Don't forget about electrical safety! All new tenancies require an electrical safety certificate, and existing tenancies required certification from April 1st, 2021. Additionally, have your electrical appliances PAT tested annually.

3. Make sure your property has working smoke alarms on each floor and carbon monoxide detectors, which are legally required. Consider installing mains interlinked smoke detectors and heat detectors in kitchens.

4. Conduct a legionella risk assessment every two years to reduce the risk of bacterial growth. You can do this yourself or enlist a professional to help.

5. Remember to obtain an Energy Performance Certificate for all advertised rental properties and ensure your property has a minimum EPC rating of E since April 2018. Also, inform your mortgage lender of your intention to rent and obtain permission before a tenant moves in.

Let it Right First Time

3 Property Presentation: Creating an Appealing Rental Space

The importance of presenting your property well cannot be understated. With attention to detail and careful consideration, you can attract high-quality tenants, ensure their satisfaction, and achieve the best possible rental income. The majority of properties today are let unfurnished, so our focus will primarily be on walls, floors, and ceilings. However, we will also discuss other aspects that can enhance the property's appeal.

Walls

Start by giving the property a fresh coat of paint throughout. Many property owners still opt for Magnolia, which means that most rental properties look similar. To set your property apart, consider incorporating a few feature walls with solid colors—nothing too bold, but rather soft tones or pastel colors that add a modern touch while maintaining a neutral palette.

Flooring

While flooring doesn't have to be expensive, it must be installed correctly. Poorly laid laminate flooring with gaps and cracks is not only unattractive but also tends to wear out quickly. Carpets and linoleum are generally more affordable options that provide a better finish and longer lifespan. Remember that tenants are responsible for any damage they cause to the flooring, subject to fair wear and tear. Typically, carpets should be replaced every five years.

Kitchen

The kitchen is one of the most important rooms in a rental property, so ensure it looks appealing. You can often revitalise a kitchen without spending a fortune by simply replacing the cupboard doors. It's also a good idea to supply basic appliances, such as an oven, fridge/freezer, and washing machine. Most tenants don't have their own appliances and providing them not only improves the presentation but also fills any unsightly gaps.

Outdoor Spaces

Make sure the property's exterior is clean and well-presented. A clean, welcoming front door is essential. Ensure any garden space is well-maintained, with trimmed grass and hedges. Consider implementing low-maintenance landscaping features to reduce upkeep.

Cleanliness

Before conducting any viewings, give the entire property a thorough cleaning, including windows. A clean, well-maintained space will leave a lasting impression on potential tenants.

Dressing

While it's not always necessary to dress an unfurnished property, doing so can create a more inviting atmosphere. If the property is furnished, invest in a few furniture items to stage the space. For instance, you could put together a dressing pack for around £100, including bedside lamps, bedspreads, fluffy cushions, and vases for flowers. This modest investment can enhance the property's overall appeal.

Remember, the condition you rent the property in is

the condition you expect it to be returned in at the end of the tenancy. Taking a few simple steps to show that you care about the property's presentation will encourage tenants to treat the space with respect.

Additional Presentation Tips

Lighting: Ensure the property has adequate lighting, both natural and artificial. Bright, well-lit spaces are more inviting and create a sense of spaciousness. Make sure all light bulbs are working and consider using energy-efficient LED bulbs.

Fixtures and Fittings: Replace any broken or outdated fixtures and fittings, such as door handles, light switches, and faucets. These small details can make a significant difference in the property's overall appearance.

Storage: Tenants appreciate ample storage space, so make the most of any built-in cupboards or shelves. If additional storage is needed, consider installing simple, inexpensive shelving units.

Window Treatments: Invest in good-quality curtains or blinds that complement the property's interior. Window treatments not only add visual interest but also provide privacy and help regulate the temperature inside the property.

Odours: Eliminate any unpleasant odours, such as those caused by dampness, pets, or tobacco smoke. Use air fresheners or scented candles to create a pleasant aroma, but avoid overpowering scents that may be off-putting to potential tenants.

6. Bathrooms: Ensure that bathrooms are clean, well-ventilated, and free of mould or mildew. Replace any damaged or stained grout, and consider updating fixtures, such as towel rails, toilet roll holders, and shower heads, for a fresh, modern look.

7. Security: Check that all doors and windows have secure, functioning locks. Install a peephole on the front door, and consider adding a security system or motion-sensor lights to enhance the property's safety.

8. Accessibility: If possible, make the property accessible to people with disabilities or mobility issues. This may include installing grab bars in bathrooms, adding ramps for wheelchair access, or widening doorways to accommodate walkers or wheelchairs.

9. Energy Efficiency: Demonstrate your commitment to sustainability by making the property more energy-efficient. This could involve adding insulation, installing double-glazed windows, or using energy-efficient

appliances.

10. Personal Touches: Add a few personal touches to the property, such as artwork, plants, or decorative pillows, to make it feel more like a home rather than a rental. These small details can create a warm, welcoming atmosphere that attracts high-quality tenants.

In conclusion, investing time and effort into the presentation of your rental property can yield significant benefits. Not only will you attract better tenants and achieve higher rental income, but you'll also establish a positive landlord-tenant relationship built on mutual respect and care for the property. Remember, every little detail counts when it comes to creating an appealing and inviting rental space. By following these guidelines and putting in the extra effort, you'll be well on your way to maximising the potential of your property and ensuring a successful rental experience.

Top tips:

1. Walls: Add a modern touch to the property by incorporating a few feature walls with solid colours that maintain a neutral palette.

2. Flooring: Choose affordable and durable flooring options like carpets and linoleum, and ensure they are installed correctly.

3. Kitchen: Revitalise the kitchen by replacing cupboard doors and supplying basic appliances, such as an oven, fridge/freezer, and washing machine.

4. Outdoor Spaces: Ensure the property's exterior is clean and well-presented, with well-maintained garden spaces.

5. Cleanliness: Before conducting any viewings, give the entire property a thorough cleaning, including windows, as a clean and well-maintained space will leave a lasting impression on potential tenants.

6. Remember to take care of small details like lighting, fixtures, storage, and odours to create a complete and appealing rental space. Additionally, consider adding personal touches like artwork and decorative pillows to make the property feel like a home. With attention to detail and careful you can attract quality tenants and achieve the best possible rental income.

4 STRATEGIC PRICING: FINDING THE RIGHT BALANCE

Achieving the optimal rental price for your property is crucial for maximising your return on investment while minimising vacancies. The right price should strike a balance between being competitive in the local market and reflecting the property's value. To determine the most strategic price for your property, you should consider the following factors and adapt your pricing strategy accordingly.

RESEARCH THE LOCAL MARKET

Before you set a price for your property, you need to familiarise yourself with the local rental market. Speak to local letting agents who have a good reputation and browse websites like Rightmove and Zoopla to gather information about rental prices in the area. Make note of the condition and size of comparable properties, and take into account any unique features that may justify a higher or lower price.

EVALUATE YOUR PROPERTY'S CONDITION

Having followed the advice from the previous chapter on property presentation, your property should be in excellent condition. If your property stands out from the competition in terms of quality, amenities, or location, you may be able to command a higher rent. However, it is essential to remain realistic and not overprice your property based on these factors alone.

BE MINDFUL OF VOID PERIODS

Overpricing your property can result in extended void periods, which can significantly impact your overall rental income. If you set your rent too high, prospective tenants may be deterred, leaving your property vacant. To illustrate this, consider the following example:

Suppose comparable two-bedroom properties in your area are renting for £550 per calendar month. You decide to list your property at £600 per month, believing it to be superior. If your property sits vacant for one month, your annual rental income will effectively be reduced to £550 per month. If it remains vacant for two months, your annual rental income will drop to £500 per month. In this scenario, the attempt to earn a higher monthly rent has cost you £1,200 in lost annual income.

MONITOR VIEWING NUMBERS AND ADJUST PRICING STRATEGY

After setting your initial asking price, it is essential to monitor the number of viewings and the feedback received from potential tenants. If you have priced your property correctly, you should see a steady stream of viewings and genuine interest. If, however, you notice a lack of interest or receive negative feedback regarding the price, you may need to adjust your pricing strategy quickly. Being proactive and responsive to market feedback can help you minimise void periods and maximise your rental income.

OFFER INCENTIVES

If you're struggling to attract tenants at your desired rental price, consider offering incentives to sweeten the deal. This could include a discounted first month's rent, a flexible lease term, or including utilities in the rental price. While these incentives may initially lower your rental income, they can help secure a tenant more quickly and reduce void periods.

MAINTAIN A COMPETITIVE EDGE

Regularly reassess your rental pricing strategy to ensure you remain competitive in the local market. As property values and rental prices fluctuate, you need to stay informed and make adjustments as necessary. A well-maintained, competitively priced property will consistently attract high-quality tenants and minimise vacancies.

In conclusion, strategic pricing is essential for the success of your rental property. By researching the local market, evaluating your property's condition, and remaining mindful of void periods, you can set an optimal rental price that maximises your return on investment. Monitoring viewing numbers and adjusting your pricing strategy based on feedback will help you respond quickly to market conditions and minimise vacancies. Implementing a pricing scale, offering incentives, and maintaining a competitive edge in the market will further enhance your property's appeal to potential tenants.

UNDERSTAND TENANT DEMOGRAPHICS

Knowing your target tenant demographic can also play a role in setting the right rental price. Consider factors such as local employment opportunities, transportation options, and nearby amenities that may be important to your target audience. Adjusting your rental price to align with the financial capabilities and preferences of your ideal tenant can help you attract the right kind of renters and reduce turnover.

CONSIDER LONG-TERM VALUE

When setting your rental price, it is important to consider the long-term value of your property investment. If your primary goal is to generate passive income, achieving the highest possible rent may not always be the best strategy. Instead, focus on maintaining a steady rental income stream and minimising vacancies by offering competitive prices, keeping your property in excellent condition, and fostering strong relationships with your tenants.

NEGOTIATE WITH POTENTIAL TENANTS

Once you have attracted potential tenants, be prepared to negotiate the rental price if necessary. If a tenant is particularly well-suited for your property and has a strong rental history, it may be worth offering a slightly lower rent to secure them as a tenant. Conversely, if a prospective tenant is willing to commit to a longer lease term or make other concessions, you might be willing to lower the rent as a trade-off.

COLLABORATE WITH A LETTING AGENT

Working with a reputable letting agent can help you navigate the complexities of rental pricing. An experienced agent can provide expert advice on local market trends, offer guidance on pricing strategy, and help you avoid common pitfalls. By leveraging their knowledge and expertise, you can set the right rental price with confidence and maximise your property's potential.

In summary, finding the right balance in rental pricing is a multifaceted process that requires research, strategy, and adaptability. By incorporating these tips and remaining responsive to market conditions, you can optimise your rental income, attract high-quality tenants, and ensure the long-term success of your property investment.

Top tips:
1. Offer multiple term options: Some tenants may prefer shorter or longer lease terms than the standard 12 months. Consider offering options for six-month or 18-month leases to appeal to a wider range of tenants.

2. Factor in management costs: When setting your rental price, be sure to include the costs of property management, such as maintenance, repairs, and tenant turnover. Failing to factor in these costs can eat into your profits and reduce your return on investment.

3. Keep an eye on the competition: Continuously monitor the prices of similar properties in your area. If you notice that comparable properties are lowering their rent, you may need to adjust your pricing strategy to remain competitive.

4. Use data and analytics: Utilise data and analytics tools to determine the best rental price for your property. These tools can provide insights into local market trends and rental demand, enabling you to set a more accurate and effective price.

5 EFFICIENT ADVERTISING: MAXIMISING EXPOSURE AND ATTRACTING TENANTS

To secure the best and quickest results for your rental property, it's essential to achieve maximum exposure. This means getting your property onto popular websites and utilising various advertising channels to reach a wide audience. While it's possible to advertise your property without an estate agent, working with an experienced professional can save you time and effort, and help you avoid potential pitfalls.

WORK WITH A LETTING AGENT

Engaging the services of a letting agent can be an effective way to advertise your property on popular websites like Rightmove and Zoopla. Although self-service agents can also get your property listed on these platforms for a small fee, working with a reputable estate agent can provide added protection against bad tenants. These tenants often try to avoid good estate agents, knowing that experienced professionals will likely uncover their deceitful intentions.

Although it might seem self-serving for an estate agent to recommend their services, the value of working with a good letting agent cannot be overstated. A reputable agent will handle the entire letting process, from advertising and viewings to contracts and paperwork. This frees up your time to focus on expanding your portfolio or enjoying other pursuits, knowing that your assets are in capable hands.

TAKE HIGH-QUALITY PHOTOS

The first impression potential tenants have of your property will come from the photos you provide in your advertisements. Invest in high-quality images that showcase your property's best features and provide an accurate representation of its condition. If necessary, consider hiring a professional photographer to ensure your photos stand out and make a lasting impression.

WRITE COMPELLING AD COPY

The text accompanying your property listing is just as important as the photos. Write compelling, informative ad copy that highlights the property's unique features and benefits, as well as local amenities and attractions. Use clear, concise language and avoid industry jargon to ensure your listing appeals to a broad audience.

UTILISE MULTIPLE ADVERTISING CHANNELS

In addition to listing your property on popular websites, consider using a range of advertising channels to maximise exposure. This may include social media platforms, local newspapers, community bulletin boards, and rental property websites. By leveraging multiple channels, you can increase the likelihood of reaching your target audience and securing a tenant quickly.

OFFER VIRTUAL TOURS

Embrace technology by offering virtual tours of your property. This can be a powerful tool in attracting tenants who may be unable or unwilling to attend in-person viewings. Virtual tours can provide a comprehensive, immersive experience that helps prospective renters visualise themselves in the space, increasing the chances of securing a tenant.

NETWORK WITH LOCAL BUSINESSES AND COMMUNITY GROUPS

Fostering relationships with local businesses, community groups, and other organisations can be an effective way to promote your property. Share information about your rental with these contacts and ask them to spread the word among their networks. This grassroots approach can complement your online advertising efforts and help you reach potential tenants who may not be actively searching online.

PROVIDE EXCELLENT CUSTOMER SERVICE

Responding promptly to inquiries, providing detailed information, and addressing any concerns will demonstrate your commitment to customer service and create a positive impression on potential tenants. By being professional and courteous, you can increase your chances of securing a tenant who will treat your property with respect and maintain a positive relationship throughout their tenancy.

MONITOR AND OPTIMISE YOUR ADVERTISING EFFORTS

Regularly review the performance of your advertisements and adjust your strategy as needed. This may include updating photos, rewriting ad copy, or exploring new advertising channels. By continually optimising your advertising efforts, you can ensure your property remains visible and appealing to prospective tenants.

To make your property more attractive and stand out from the competition, consider offering incentives to prospective tenants. These may include reduced rent for the first month, a waived security deposit, or gift cards for local businesses. Incentives can make your property more appealing and encourage potential tenants to choose your property over others.

PROMOTE ENERGY EFFICIENCY AND SUSTAINABILITY

Highlight any energy-efficient features or sustainable aspects of your property, such as solar panels, energy-efficient appliances, or a well-insulated building. These features can attract environmentally conscious tenants and potentially reduce utility costs, making your property more attractive in the long run.

ADVERTISE TO YOUR TARGET MARKET

Identify the type of tenant you want to attract and tailor your advertising efforts accordingly. For example, if you want to target young professionals, emphasise the property's proximity to public transportation and local amenities. If you're looking to attract families, highlight nearby schools and parks. By targeting your ideal tenant, you can improve the chances of securing a tenant who is a good fit for your property.

REQUEST TESTIMONIALS FROM CURRENT OR PAST TENANTS

Positive reviews from satisfied tenants can help build trust and credibility with prospective renters. Ask current or past tenants to provide testimonials that you can include in your advertising materials. These reviews can offer valuable insight into the living experience at your property and encourage potential tenants to consider renting from you.

OFFER FLEXIBLE LEASE TERMS

Consider offering flexible lease terms, such as shorter leases or the option to renew month-to-month. This flexibility can be appealing to potential tenants who may be uncertain about their long-term plans. By accommodating different needs, you can broaden your pool of potential renters and increase the likelihood of securing a tenant.

MAINTAIN A STRONG ONLINE PRESENCE

A professional and informative website can be an excellent tool for showcasing your property and attracting tenants. Include high-quality photos, detailed property descriptions, and information about the application process. Also, consider creating a blog or social media presence to share updates, news, and other relevant information that can engage your target audience and build your reputation as a trustworthy landlord.

By implementing these strategies and focusing on efficient advertising, you can maximise your property's exposure and attract high-quality tenants quickly. Whether you choose to work with an estate agent or handle the advertising process yourself, taking a proactive and strategic approach to advertising will help ensure the success of your rental property.

Top tips:

1. Work with an agent to save time and effort, and maximise exposure on popular websites. A reputable agent can handle the entire letting process, from advertising and viewings to contracts and paperwork.

2. Provide quality photos that showcase your property's best features and provide an accurate representation of its condition. Consider hiring a professional photographer to ensure your photos stand out and make a lasting impression.

3. Write compelling ad copy that highlights the property's unique features and benefits, as well as local amenities and attractions. Use clear, concise language and avoid jargon to ensure your listing appeals to a broad audience.

4. Utilise multiple advertising channels, including social media platforms, community bulletin boards, rental property websites, and virtual tours to increase exposure and attract potential tenants.

5. Foster relationships with local businesses and other organisations to promote your property through word-of-mouth. Provide excellent customer service by responding promptly to inquiries, providing detailed information, and addressing any concerns to increase the chances of securing a good tenant.

6 CONDUCTING SUCCESSFUL VIEWINGS: CREATING DEMAND AND SELECTING THE BEST TENANTS

Creating demand for your rental property is key to a successful viewing experience. When you have potential tenants eagerly competing for your property, you have the opportunity to choose the best fit for your space. By following the steps in previous chapters, you've set the stage for a successful viewing experience. In this chapter, we will explore strategies for conducting viewings that generate demand and help you select the best tenants.

SCHEDULE VIEWINGS STRATEGICALLY

Don't leave the scheduling of viewings entirely up to potential tenants. Instead, set specific viewing slots and encourage interested parties to attend during those times. Aim to schedule viewings no more than a week in advance and preferably on weekends, as the best tenants are often at work during the week.

CONDUCT GROUP VIEWINGS

Organise group viewings by having all interested parties visit the property at the same time. This approach creates a sense of urgency and demand, as potential tenants can see that others are interested in the property as well. Limit the viewing slot to about 15 minutes to maintain this sense of urgency.

PREPARE THE PROPERTY

Arrive early to prepare the property for viewings. Open windows to let in fresh air, turn on all lights to create a bright atmosphere, and adjust the heating to ensure the space is warm and welcoming. Be mindful of striking a balance between air circulation and maintaining a comfortable temperature.

MANAGE APPLICANT EXPECTATIONS

As applicants arrive, apologise for the number of people and explain that the property is in high demand and likely to be rented quickly. Inform them that if they wish to secure the property, they will need to apply promptly, as applications will be processed on a first-come, first-served basis.

PROVIDE APPLICATION OPTIONS

Offer both online and paper application forms to accommodate various preferences. Make the application process as seamless as possible to encourage potential tenants to submit their applications promptly.

FOLLOW UP AFTER VIEWINGS

After the viewing, reach out to potential tenants to thank them for their interest and inquire if they have any questions or concerns. This follow-up communication can help keep your property top-of-mind and encourage applicants to move forward with the application process.

EVALUATE APPLICATIONS

Once you have received multiple applications, carefully evaluate each one to determine the best fit for your property. Consider factors such as rental history, credit score, employment status, and references to make an informed decision.

COMMUNICATE WITH APPLICANTS

Keep all applicants informed of the status of their application and notify them promptly if they have been selected or if the property has been rented to someone else. This communication demonstrates professionalism and maintains a positive relationship with potential tenants who may be interested in future rental opportunities.

LEARN FROM EACH VIEWING

After each viewing, take a moment to reflect on what went well and what could be improved. Use this information to refine your approach and enhance the viewing experience for future applicants.

BUILD A WAIT LIST

If your property generates a significant amount of interest, consider maintaining a wait list of potential tenants who were not selected. This list can be useful for future vacancies, saving time and effort in the tenant search process.

By implementing these strategies and conducting

successful viewings, you can create demand for your rental property and select the best tenants to occupy your space. When managed effectively, a well-executed viewing process can result in a win-win situation for both you and your new tenants.

Top tips:

1. Schedule viewings strategically: set specific viewing slots and encourage interested parties to attend during those times, no more than a week in advance and preferably on weekends.

2. Conduct group viewings: organise group viewings to create a sense of urgency and demand, and limit the viewing slot to about 15 minutes to maintain this sense of urgency.

3. Prepare the property: arrive early to prepare the property for viewings, open windows to let in fresh air, turn on all lights to create a bright atmosphere, and adjust the heating to ensure the space is warm and welcoming.

4. Manage applicant expectations: inform applicants that the property is in high demand and likely to be rented quickly, and that they will need to apply promptly to secure the property.

5. Follow up after viewings: reach out to potential tenants to thank them for their interest and inquire if they have any questions or concerns. This follow-up communication can help keep your property top-of-mind and encourage applicants to move forward with the application process.

7 TENANT SCREENING AND REFERENCING: ENSURING A GOOD FIT

Selecting the right tenant is crucial to a successful landlord-tenant relationship. While most tenants are responsible and reliable, there are some individuals who may try to cheat the system. Conducting thorough screening and referencing checks is essential for minimising the risk of problems down the line. In this chapter, we will explore various aspects of tenant screening and referencing, and provide tips for conducting effective checks.

LANDLORD REFERENCE

A landlord reference from the current and, if possible, the previous landlord, is an invaluable resource for understanding the tenant's rental history. Keep in mind that the current landlord may not provide a completely accurate reference if they want to get rid of a problematic tenant. However, a previous landlord will likely offer more reliable information.

To ensure that the reference is genuine, verify the landlord's identity by conducting a Land Registry check and requesting a copy of the existing tenancy agreement. These measures can help confirm the authenticity of the information provided.

EMPLOYER REFERENCE

Obtaining an employer reference is essential for confirming the tenant's employment status, the nature of their contract, and their declared salary. Request the reference via email, as this provides a paper trail and allows you to confirm that the reference is coming from a legitimate company email address.

To further verify the information, conduct a follow-up phone call with the company and ask to speak to the manager or HR department. Be aware that large organizations, such as the police or the NHS, may require written consent from the tenant before providing any information.

CREDIT CHECKS

Credit checks are one of the most reliable measures of a tenant's financial responsibility. Tenants who consistently fail to pay their rent are often similarly negligent with other bills, which will be reflected in their credit report. Ensure that you are conducting the credit check on the correct individual by verifying their identity beforehand.

ID CHECKS – Including Right to rent checks.

Request photographic ID, ideally a passport, and a utility bill dated within the last three months. In addition to verifying the tenant's identity, you are legally required to conduct Right to Rent checks to ensure that the tenant is eligible to live in the UK. The specific requirements for these checks may change over time, so it is best to consult the government website or contact a knowledgeable professional for the most up-to-date information. The UK government requires non UK Nationals to provide a share code which you must verify here: https://www.gov.uk/view-right-to-rent

ADDITIONAL CHECKS AND CONSIDERATIONS

Consider conducting additional checks, such as social media searches and online background checks, to gain a more comprehensive understanding of the tenant's character and lifestyle. Additionally, assess the tenant's monthly employed income, which should generally be at least 2.5 times the monthly rent, to ensure that they can comfortably afford the rental payments.

DOCUMENTATION AND ORGANIZATION

Keep thorough records of all tenant screening and referencing checks, including copies of references, credit reports, and identification documents. These records may prove invaluable in the event of disputes or legal issues down the line.

COMMUNICATION AND TRANSPARENCY

Maintain open communication with potential tenants throughout the screening and referencing process. Be transparent about the checks being conducted and the information being collected, and encourage applicants to provide any necessary documentation or consent promptly.

ONGOING MONITORING AND EVALUATION

Once the tenant has been selected and has moved into the property, continue to monitor and evaluate their performance as a tenant. Regular inspections and open communication can help identify and address any issues before they escalate.

LEARNING FROM EXPERIENCE

Reflect on your tenant screening and referencing experiences, identifying areas for improvement and refining your approach as needed. By continuously learning from past experiences, you can enhance your tenant selection process and minimise the risk of problems in the future.

UTILISING PROFESSIONAL SERVICES

If you find the tenant screening and referencing process overwhelming or time-consuming, consider engaging the services of a reputable letting agent or property management company. These professionals can conduct thorough checks on your behalf, ensuring that you select the best possible tenants for your property.

DEVELOPING A CONSISTENT CRITERIA

Establish a consistent set of criteria for evaluating potential tenants. By maintaining uniform standards, you can ensure that your tenant selection process is fair, unbiased, and effective. This consistency also helps minimise the risk of inadvertently violating anti-discrimination laws.

MAINTAINING FLEXIBILITY AND EMPATHY

While it is essential to conduct thorough tenant screening and referencing, also remember to maintain a degree of flexibility and empathy. Circumstances can change, and an individual's past behavior may not necessarily dictate their future actions. Strike a balance between protecting your interests and providing opportunities for tenants who may have experienced past difficulties.

NETWORKING AND INFORMATION SHARING

Connect with other landlords, property managers, and industry professionals to share insights, experiences, and best practices related to tenant screening and referencing. Networking can help you stay informed about emerging trends, new tools, and potential pitfalls to avoid.

STAYING CURRENT WITH LEGISLATION AND REGULATIONS

Ensure that you remain up to date with any changes in legislation or regulations related to tenant screening and referencing. By staying informed, you can ensure that your processes remain compliant and legally sound.

EDUCATING YOURSELF AND SEEKING EXPERT ADVICE

Invest in your own knowledge and understanding of tenant screening and referencing by attending workshops, seminars, and training sessions. Additionally, consider seeking advice from legal and industry experts to ensure that your approach is comprehensive and effective.

In conclusion, tenant screening and referencing are critical aspects of managing rental properties, and conducting thorough checks can significantly reduce the risk of encountering problematic tenants. By following the guidelines outlined in this chapter and continuously refining your approach, you can improve your tenant selection process and foster successful landlord-tenant relationships. Remember that while screening and referencing are essential, maintaining open communication, flexibility, and empathy can also contribute to a positive experience for both you and your tenants.

Top tips:

1. Develop a set of standards for evaluating potential and apply them uniformly to all applicants. This can help prevent any allegations of discrimination and ensure that you select the best possible tenant for your property.

2. Be open and transparent with applicants about the tenant referencing process, and explain why each check is necessary. Encourage them to provide any necessary information or documentation promptly to ensure a smooth and efficient process.

3. Conduct thorough checks on potential tenants, including landlord and employer references, credit checks, and ID checks.

4. Keep thorough records of all tenant screening and referencing checks, including copies of references, credit reports, and identification documents. These records can be invaluable in the event of disputes or legal issues down the line.

5. If you find the tenant screening and referencing process overwhelming or time-consuming, consider seeking the services of a reputable letting agent. They can conduct thorough checks on your behalf and ensure that you select the best possible tenants for your property.

8 CONTRACTS AND INVENTORIES: PROTECTING YOUR INTERESTS

Creating a comprehensive contract and inventory is essential for protecting your interests as a landlord. This chapter will delve into the importance of each component, as well as provide guidelines for drafting and implementing these documents.

A. ASSURED SHORTHOLD TENANCY AGREEMENTS

Types of Tenancy Agreements
The most common type of tenancy agreement is the Assured Shorthold Tenancy (AST). There are other agreement types available, but the AST is typically the most suitable for most rental situations.

Another frequently used agreement is the lodging license, which is only applicable if you, the landlord, reside at the property. Be cautious not to misuse this license for room lets without your residency, as it would not be enforceable in court.

Terms and Duration

The minimum duration for an AST is six months. Many landlords opt for this term, but you may consider offering a 12-month agreement with a 6-month break clause for added security for both parties. Avoid extending the agreement beyond three years, as this would necessitate a different type of contract.

It is crucial to note that an AST can be a verbal agreement, but it is advisable to have a written contract to provide proof of the agreed terms in case of legal disputes. Various templates are available online, or you can consult with a legal professional or letting agent for assistance.

Periodic Tenancies

Upon the expiration of a fixed-term tenancy, the agreement automatically converts into a statutory periodic tenancy. This allows the tenant to remain in the property under the original contract terms without committing to a new fixed period. Tenants are required to provide one month's notice if they wish to vacate, while landlords must give a two-month notice to regain possession of the property.

B. INVENTORY MANAGEMENT

Importance of a Photographic Inventory
It is essential to create a detailed photographic inventory of your property before renting it out. This can be done independently or through a letting agent or inventory clerk. A comprehensive inventory provides evidence of the property's condition, which can be crucial in resolving disputes or claiming damages at the end of a tenancy.

Assisting Tenant Recall

A photographic inventory can also serve as a reminder for tenants regarding the property's initial condition. As some tenancies may span several years, it is helpful to have a record of the property's state upon move-in to clarify expectations upon move-out.

Managing Wear and Tear

Long-term tenants may cause natural wear and tear on the property, which should be expected and accounted for as a landlord. Establishing a balance between maintaining the property and accommodating for reasonable wear is crucial. Clear communication with tenants about expectations upon their departure can help ensure a smooth transition and minimise disputes over the return of the security deposit.

C. CONTRACT AND INVENTORY SIGNING

Key Elements of a Tenancy Agreement

A tenancy agreement should include the rent amount, security deposit, duration of the agreement, tenant's name and addresses, landlord's name and address (known as section 47 and section 48, and legally required), and signatures of both parties.

Timing of Signing

The tenancy agreement and inventory should be signed before the tenant takes possession of the property. This ensures that both parties are in agreement on the terms and conditions of the rental and the property's condition at the start of the tenancy.

In conclusion, crafting a solid contract and inventory is critical to protecting your interests as a landlord. By following the guidelines outlined in this chapter, you can develop comprehensive and legally sound documents that minimise disputes and safeguard your investment. Remember that communication and transparency are essential for fostering a positive landlord-tenant relationship, and maintaining clear expectations from the outset can help ensure a successful and stress-free rental experience.

D. UPDATING AND RENEWING AGREEMENTS

Regular Reviews

It is crucial to review the tenancy agreement periodically to ensure its terms remain relevant and compliant with current regulations. Regular reviews can help identify any necessary updates or amendments to the agreement, such as rent increases or changes in legislation.

Renewing Fixed-Term Agreements

When a fixed-term agreement is nearing its end, you may choose to renew the tenancy for another fixed period. In this case, ensure that any updates or changes to the terms are clearly outlined and agreed upon by both parties before signing the new contract.

E. DEALING WITH BREACHES OF CONTRACT

Addressing Issues Early

As a landlord, it is crucial to address any breaches of contract promptly and professionally. Ignoring or delaying action on issues may lead to further complications and potential legal disputes down the line.

Communication and Resolution

In most cases, clear communication and negotiation with the tenant can help resolve breaches of contract without the need for legal intervention. Ensure you understand the terms of the agreement and are prepared to discuss and negotiate a fair resolution with the tenant.

Legal Action

If a breach of contract cannot be resolved through communication and negotiation, you may need to take legal action. Consult with a legal professional or letting agent to determine the appropriate course of action based on your situation and the terms of your tenancy agreement.

Top tips:

1. If you are new to renting out properties, consider seeking professional assistance from a letting agent. They can provide guidance on drafting legally sound contracts and inventories, ensuring you protect your interests and comply with regulations.

2. When drafting contracts and inventories, be as thorough and detailed as possible. This can help prevent disputes and misunderstandings down the line, and serve as evidence in legal proceedings if necessary.

3. Regularly review and update your contracts and inventories to ensure they remain compliant with regulations. This can help prevent potential legal issues and ensure that both parties are aware of their rights and responsibilities.

4. Maintain clear and open communication with your tenants throughout the tenancy, including during the signing of contracts and inventories. This can help foster a positive relationship and minimise disputes.

5. If a breach of contract occurs, address the issue promptly. Ignoring or delaying action may only lead to further complications and potential legal disputes. Communication and negotiation can often resolve issues, but legal action may be necessary in some cases.

9 MANAGING RENT AND DEPOSITS: FINANCIAL MATTERS

Effectively managing rent and deposits is an essential aspect of a successful landlord-tenant relationship. In this chapter, we will cover the best practices for collecting and managing rent and deposits, ensuring compliance with legal requirements, and maintaining a smooth financial process.

A. TIMING OF RENT AND DEPOSIT COLLECTION

Deposit Collection

Once the tenant's credit checks have been completed and approved, you should request the deposit. This ensures that the tenant is committed to the property and reduces the likelihood of last-minute cancellations.

Rent Collection

After the tenancy agreement has been signed, collect the rent from the tenant. The rent should be collected in advance of the tenant taking possession of the property to ensure you have cleared funds.

B. LIMITATIONS AND PROTECTION OF DEPOSITS

Maximum Deposit Amount

The maximum deposit you can collect is equivalent to five weeks' rent, regardless of any additional considerations such as pets or other factors.

Deposit Protection

Deposits must be protected within 30 days of receipt. There are several authorised firms that provide deposit protection services, such as The Tenancy Deposits Scheme (TDS). The TDS offers both custodial (they hold the deposit) and insured (you hold the deposit) schemes. Visit tenancydepositscheme.com for more information.

C. PRESCRIBED INFORMATION AND COMPLIANCE

Providing Prescribed Information

You must issue the prescribed information document to the tenant within 30 days of receiving the deposit. Failure to do so may impede your ability to issue a Section 21 notice and evict your tenant, and you could face fines of up to three times the deposit amount for each offense.

Providing Additional Documents

Along with the prescribed information, ensure you send the Energy Performance Certificate (EPC), gas safety certificate, and "How to Rent" booklet to the tenant. Combining these documents into one communication can streamline the process and ensure you fulfill all legal requirements.

A competent estate agent can help you manage these documents and ensure compliance.

D. ESTATE AGENT REQUIREMENTS AND RESPONSIBILITIES

Client Bank Accounts

Estate agents must have a separate client bank account to accept rents and deposits, ensuring that funds are managed securely and separately from the agent's own finances.

Client Money Protection Insurance

All agents are required to have client money protection insurance. This insurance safeguards your funds in case of mismanagement or other issues with the agent.

ARLA Propertymark Registered Agents

To ensure the highest level of protection and service, look for agents registered with ARLA Propertymark. These agents are required to have client money protection insurance and adhere to strict professional standards. Make sure you request a copy of their insurance certificate before entrusting them with your funds.

E. SETTING UP RENT COLLECTION PROCEDURES

Clear Payment Expectations

Establish clear expectations for rent payment, including the due date, preferred payment method, and any potential late fees. Communicate these expectations to the tenant before they move in, and include them in the tenancy agreement.

Rent Collection Methods

Choose a rent collection method that works best for you and your tenant. Common methods include direct debit, standing orders, or electronic transfers. Ensure that your chosen method is secure and easily trackable.

Monitoring Rent Payments

Regularly monitor rent payments to ensure timely receipt. If a tenant is consistently late or misses payments, address the issue promptly and professionally to avoid further complications.

F. HANDLING DEPOSIT DISPUTES AND RETURNS

Check-Out Inspections

Upon the end of the tenancy, conduct a thorough check-out inspection to assess the property's condition and compare it to the initial inventory. This will help determine any deductions from the deposit due to damages or cleaning requirements.

Fair Wear and Tear

Keep in mind that some wear and tear is to be expected, especially in long-term tenancies. Be reasonable when assessing damages, and consider the age and condition of items in the property when determining whether a deduction is warranted.

Communicating Deductions

If deductions are necessary, clearly communicate the reasons and amounts to the tenant. Provide evidence, such as photographs and receipts, to support your claims. Open communication can help prevent disputes and maintain a positive landlord-tenant relationship.

Deposit Return Timeline

Once the final deductions have been agreed upon, return the remaining deposit to the tenant promptly. Be aware of the time frames outlined by your chosen deposit protection scheme, as failure to return the deposit within the specified time frame could result in penalties.

G. PREVENTING FUTURE ISSUES

Regular Property Inspections

Conducting regular property inspections can help you identify potential issues before they escalate. By keeping an eye on the property's condition, you can address any maintenance needs or tenant concerns in a timely manner.

Open Communication with Tenants

Maintain open lines of communication with your tenants to encourage them to report any issues or concerns. This proactive approach can help prevent problems from escalating and contribute to a positive landlord-tenant relationship.

Review and Update Tenancy Agreements

Regularly review and update your tenancy agreements to ensure they are in line with current legislation and best practices. This can help protect your interests and minimise potential issues in the future.

H. CONCLUSION

Effectively managing rent and deposits is crucial for

maintaining a successful landlord-tenant relationship and ensuring the financial stability of your property investment. By following the best practices outlined in this chapter, you can navigate the financial aspects of renting with confidence and protect your interests. Remember to stay informed about current legislation and seek the help of a reputable estate agent or professional when needed.

Top tips:

1. **Collect deposits and rent on time:** Collect the deposit as soon as the tenant's credit checks are completed and approved. Collect rent in advance of the tenant taking possession of the property to ensure you have cleared funds.

2. **Understand limitations and protection of deposits:** Ensure you collect a maximum deposit amount of 5 weeks' rent and protect it within 30 days of receipt. Use authorised firms such as The Tenancy Deposits Scheme for deposit protection.

3. **Fulfill legal requirements:** Issue the prescribed information document to the tenant within 30 days of receiving the deposit, along with the Energy Performance Certificate, gas safety certificate, and "How to Rent" booklet.

4. **Set up rent collection procedures:** Establish clear payment expectations, choose a secure payment method, and monitor rent payments regularly.

5. **Handle deposit disputes and returns professionally:** Conduct a thorough check-out inspection, communicate deductions clearly, and return the remaining deposit promptly. Regular property inspections and open communication with tenants can prevent future issues.

10 THE MOVE-IN PROCESS: ENSURING A SMOOTH TRANSITION

A well-executed move-in process is essential to starting your landlord-tenant relationship on the right foot. Taking the time to ensure a smooth transition will help you avoid potential issues down the line and contribute to a positive experience for both parties.

A. PREPARING THE PROPERTY

Clean and Tidy

Ensure the property is clean and presentable before the tenants move in. This includes conducting any necessary repairs and maintenance, as well as ensuring all appliances and fixtures are in good working order.

Safety Checks

Carry out all required safety checks, such as gas and electrical safety inspections, smoke and carbon monoxide detectors, and ensure all relevant certificates are up to date. Providing a safe living environment for your tenants is both a legal obligation and a moral responsibility.

B. WELCOMING THE TENANTS

Arrange a Move-in Appointment

Schedule a move-in appointment with your tenants to walk them through the property, hand over the keys, and complete any necessary paperwork. This appointment should be scheduled at a mutually convenient time, allowing ample time for a thorough walk through of the property.

Prepare a Welcome Pack

Create a welcome pack for your tenants, containing useful information about the property and the local area. This may include emergency contact numbers, appliance manuals, instructions for operating the heating and hot water systems, information on local amenities and services, and any other relevant information that may be helpful to your tenants.

C. CONDUCTING THE MOVE-IN INSPECTION

Review the Inventory

Go through the inventory with your tenants, making sure they understand the contents and agree with the listed condition of the property and its contents. Both parties should sign and date the inventory to confirm its accuracy.

Take Meter Readings

During the move-in inspection, take readings for electricity, gas, and water meters. Record these readings on the inventory, and take photos for added documentation. Advise your tenants to set up their accounts with the utility suppliers and the local council.

Demonstrate Important Features

Take the time to show your tenants how the heating and hot water systems work, and test them if possible while you are at the property. Show them the location of the stopcock in case of emergencies, and explain what to do and who to contact in such situations. Familiarising your tenants with these essential features can help prevent future issues and ensure they feel comfortable in their new home.

D. COMPLETING THE MOVE-IN PROCESS

Handing Over the Keys

Once you have completed the move-in inspection and all necessary paperwork, hand over the keys to your tenants. Provide them with enough sets of keys for all adult occupants, and keep a spare set for yourself in case of emergencies.

Updating Contact Information

Ensure your tenants have all the necessary contact information for you or your managing agent. This includes phone numbers, email addresses, and any preferred methods of communication. If you have a managing agent, encourage your tenants to contact the agent directly with any issues or concerns, rather than reaching out to you directly.

E. ONGOING COMMUNICATION AND SUPPORT

Be Proactive

In the early stages of the tenancy, maintain open lines of communication with your tenants. Check in with them to ensure they are settling in well and address any issues or concerns that may arise.

Provide Ongoing Support

Be available to provide support and guidance to your tenants throughout their tenancy. This may include answering questions, addressing maintenance requests, or providing information on local services and amenities. By demonstrating your commitment to your tenants' well-being, you can foster a positive landlord-tenant relationship that benefits both parties.

In conclusion, a successful move-in process lays the foundation for a strong landlord-tenant relationship and ensures that both parties start off on the right foot. By taking the time to prepare the property, welcome your tenants, conduct a thorough move-in inspection, and provide ongoing support, you can create a positive living environment and minimise the potential for issues down the line.

F. RECORD-KEEPING AND DOCUMENTATION

Maintain Organised Records

Keep organised records of all important documents, including the signed tenancy agreement, inventory, safety certificates, and any correspondence between you and your tenants. Good record-keeping practices will ensure that you have all the necessary information at hand in the event of a dispute or legal issue.

Update and Review Documents Regularly

Regularly review your records and update them as needed, such as when you renew safety certificates or conduct periodic inspections. This ensures that you have an accurate and up-to-date account of the property's condition and any changes that may have occurred during the tenancy.

G. PERIODIC INSPECTIONS AND MAINTENANCE

Schedule Regular Inspections

Conduct periodic inspections of the property to ensure it remains in good condition and to identify any maintenance issues that may need attention. Communicate with your tenants in advance to schedule these inspections at a mutually convenient time, and provide them with the required notice as stipulated in your tenancy agreement.

Address Maintenance Issues Promptly

Respond to maintenance requests and issues in a timely manner, as this demonstrates your commitment to providing a safe and comfortable living environment for your tenants. Keeping on top of maintenance not only keeps your tenants happy but also helps to maintain the value and condition of your property.

H. END-OF-TENANCY PROCEDURES

Conduct a Final Inspection

When your tenants decide to move out, schedule a final inspection to assess the property's condition and compare it to the original inventory. This will help you determine whether any deductions need to be made from the security deposit to cover damages or cleaning costs.

Returning the Security Deposit

Once the final inspection is complete and any necessary deductions have been agreed upon, return the remaining security deposit to your tenants within the required time frame. Ensure that you follow the correct procedures for returning the deposit, as outlined by your chosen deposit protection scheme.

Prepare for the Next Tenancy

After your tenants have vacated the property, take the necessary steps to prepare for the next tenancy. This may include conducting repairs or maintenance, updating safety certificates, and cleaning the property thoroughly.

In summary, a well-planned and executed move-in process sets the stage for a successful tenancy and helps to create a positive experience for both landlords and tenants. By focusing on key areas such as property preparation, welcoming tenants, conducting inspections, and providing ongoing support, you can help ensure a smooth transition and a harmonious landlord-tenant relationship.

Top tips:

1. Prepare the property by ensuring it is clean and tidy, and all necessary safety checks are carried out, such as gas and electrical safety inspections, smoke and carbon monoxide detectors, and relevant certificates are up to date.

2. Schedule a move-in appointment and create a welcome pack for your tenants that includes useful information about the property and local area.

3. Conduct a thorough move-in inspection by reviewing the inventory, taking meter readings, and demonstrating important features of the property such as the heating and hot water systems.

4. Hand over the keys and update contact information for ongoing communication and support, including being proactive in addressing any issues or concerns.

5. Maintain organised records and documentation, schedule regular inspections and maintenance, and follow end-of-tenancy procedures to ensure a smooth transition to the next tenancy.

11 REGULAR INSPECTIONS: MAINTAINING YOUR PROPERTY AND ADDRESSING CONCERNS

Conducting regular inspections of your rental property is crucial for ensuring its proper maintenance and addressing any issues that may arise. Generally, inspections should be carried out twice per year, as more frequent visits may be perceived as an invasion of the tenant's right to quiet enjoyment of the property.

A. SCHEDULING THE FIRST INSPECTION

It is recommended that the first inspection is carried out within 1-2 months of the tenancy commencement. While many landlords may opt for a 3-month interval, an earlier inspection can be beneficial for both parties in addressing any potential issues early on.

One major concern for landlords is the potential misuse of their property, such as the illegal cultivation of marijuana. By informing tenants that an inspection will be conducted within the first month, you can deter individuals with nefarious intentions from renting your property. Early inspections help protect your investment and maintain the property's integrity.

B. ONGOING INSPECTIONS AND FOLLOW-UPS

After the initial inspection, you may consider scheduling subsequent inspections at 6-month intervals, with occasional phone check-ins to ensure everything is running smoothly. In cases where maintenance or safety certificates are required, you can ask the contractor to assess the property's overall condition and report back to you.

If any issues arise during an inspection, it's essential to request that they be addressed promptly and schedule a follow-up inspection to verify that the necessary repairs or improvements have been made.

C. IMPORTANCE OF TIMELY REPAIRS AND MAINTENANCE

Maintaining a well-kept property benefits both landlords and tenants. Addressing repairs swiftly not only demonstrates your commitment to providing a comfortable living environment but also helps prevent more extensive and costly issues down the line.

Tenants have the right to contact their local Environmental Health department if repairs are not attended to promptly. Failure to address these concerns could result in enforcement orders mandating additional repairs, and the department may even undertake the work themselves, adding a significant charge on top of the repair bill.

D. INSPECTION CHECKLIST

To ensure that your inspections are thorough and consistent, consider creating an inspection checklist that covers the following areas:

Exterior: Inspect the property's exterior for any signs of damage, wear and tear, or maintenance needs, such as gutters, roofing, or paintwork.

Interior: Examine the property's interior for any signs of damage, wear and tear, or maintenance needs, such as flooring, walls, ceilings, or windows.

Appliances and Systems: Check all appliances, heating, ventilation, and air conditioning systems for proper functioning and any signs of wear or malfunction.

Safety Features: Ensure that all safety features, such as smoke detectors, carbon monoxide detectors, and fire extinguishers, are in good working order and meet legal requirements.

General Cleanliness: Assess the overall cleanliness of the property and ensure that tenants are maintaining a reasonable standard of cleanliness to prevent long-term damage or pest infestations.

Unreported Maintenance Issues: Identify any unreported maintenance issues that may require attention, such as leaking pipes, damaged fixtures, or malfunctioning appliances.

E. DOCUMENTING INSPECTIONS

Proper documentation of inspections is essential for maintaining accurate records and addressing any disputes or legal issues that may arise. Consider taking photographs of any issues discovered during the inspection and keeping detailed notes on the property's condition and any required repairs or

improvements.

F. COMMUNICATION WITH TENANTS

Maintaining open lines of communication with your tenants is crucial for fostering a positive landlord-tenant relationship. Discuss any concerns or issues that arise during the inspection and work collaboratively to address them. By showing your commitment to maintaining a safe and comfortable living environment, you can build trust with your tenants and ensure a smoother rental experience for all parties involved.

G. THE ROLE OF A PROPERTY MANAGEMENT AGENCY

If you prefer not to manage the inspection process yourself or lack the necessary time or expertise, you can consider hiring a property management agency to conduct regular inspections on your behalf. A reputable property management company can help ensure that your property is well-maintained and that any issues are addressed promptly and professionally.

H. DEALING WITH NON-COMPLIANT TENANTS

In cases where tenants fail to address issues identified during inspections or consistently neglect their responsibilities, it may be necessary to take further action. Depending on the severity of the situation, you may need to issue formal warnings, make arrangements for repairs at the tenant's expense, or, in extreme cases, initiate eviction proceedings. Be sure to familiarise yourself with local laws and regulations regarding tenant-landlord disputes and consult with a legal professional if necessary.

I. MAINTAINING POSITIVE RELATIONSHIPS WITH TENANTS

While regular inspections are essential for protecting your property investment, it's also important to foster positive relationships with your tenants. Here are some tips for maintaining good rapport with your tenants:

Respect their privacy: Give your tenants ample notice before conducting inspections and avoid scheduling them too frequently.

Be responsive: Address maintenance issues and concerns promptly to show your commitment to their well-being and comfort.

Be fair and transparent: Communicate clearly with your tenants about any issues found during inspections and work together to find mutually agreeable solutions.

Foster open communication: Encourage tenants to report any problems or concerns they may have and maintain open lines of communication throughout the tenancy.

In conclusion, regular property inspections are a vital aspect of managing rental properties. By conducting thorough, well-documented inspections and addressing any issues that arise, you can protect your investment, maintain a well-kept property, and foster positive relationships with your tenants. Whether you choose to manage inspections yourself or enlist the help of a property management agency, staying diligent in this area will pay dividends in the long run.

Top tips:

1. Schedule the first inspection within 1-2 months of tenancy commencement to address potential issues early on and protect your investment from misuse or damage.

2. Create an inspection checklist to ensure thorough and consistent inspections of the property's exterior, interior, appliances and systems, safety features, general cleanliness, and unreported maintenance issues.

3. Properly document inspections, taking photographs of issues discovered and keeping detailed notes on the property's condition and any required repairs or improvements.

4. Foster open communication with tenants, addressing maintenance issues and concerns promptly and working together to find mutually agreeable solutions.

5. Consider hiring a reputable property management agency if you lack the time or expertise to manage inspections yourself, or if you prefer to have a third-party handle this aspect of property management.

12 THE MOVE-OUT PROCESS: ENDING THE TENANCY ON A POSITIVE NOTE

A. INTRODUCTION

Every tenancy will eventually come to an end. When this occurs, it is essential to follow the proper procedures to ensure a smooth and positive transition for both you and your tenant. This chapter will guide you through the move-out process and provide tips for reducing void periods and handling potential disputes.

B. PREPARING FOR THE MOVE-OUT

Notice Periods and Advertising: Upon receiving or giving notice, it is crucial to begin advertising the property as soon as possible to minimise void periods. Ideally, you should start advertising no sooner than one month before the property's available date. Tenants are typically required to provide one month's notice, while landlords must give two months' notice.

Section 21 and Section 8 Notices: If you are giving notice, you must use a Section 21 form for standard notice at the end of a fixed-term tenancy. For breaches of tenancy, a Section 8 notice should be used. Please note that tenants may not vacate the property on the agreed date even after being issued a notice requiring possession (a Section 21 notice). Enforcement can only be arranged through the courts.

C. COMMUNICATING WITH YOUR TENANT

Upon confirming the move-out date, send your tenant a letter or email detailing the move-out process and reminding them of their responsibilities, such as cleaning the property and repairing any damage. Open communication is key to ensuring a smooth move-out process for both parties.

D. THE FINAL INSPECTION

Schedule a meeting with your tenant at the property on the move-out date. Conduct a thorough inspection, take meter readings, and obtain a forwarding address for the tenant. Compare the property's current condition with the initial inventory to identify any discrepancies or issues that need to be addressed.

E. HANDLING THE DEPOSIT

The deposit should be refunded to the tenant once you are satisfied that the property is in acceptable condition. If there are any disputes regarding the property's condition, allow the tenant an opportunity to rectify the problem. Should the tenant fail to resolve the issue, you may make a deduction from the deposit, provided that valid estimates are obtained to indicate the exact cost of repair.

F. DEALING WITH DISPUTES

In cases where an agreement cannot be reached between the landlord and tenant, the Alternative Dispute Resolution Service (provided by The TDS) may be used. Their decision will be final. It is crucial to never commit to releasing the deposit on the move-out day and to advise any possible deductions within five days of the tenancy's end. The actual amount may take some time to determine, as estimates and additional information may be needed.

G. A SEAMLESS MOVE-OUT PROCESS

The move-out process is a crucial part of the rental cycle and requires careful planning and execution. By following the steps outlined in this chapter, you can create a positive experience for both you and your tenant, minimising potential disputes and ensuring a smooth transition.

H. RESOURCES AND FURTHER READING

For a more in-depth discussion of the checkout and dispute process, consider reading "Check it Right First Time," a comprehensive guide written by my wife that delves into the intricacies of this crucial aspect of property management.

I. MOVING FORWARD

With the move-out process complete, it is time to prepare for your next tenant. By repeating the steps outlined in this guide, you can continue to successfully manage your rental property and ensure a positive experience for all parties involved.

Top tips:

1. Advertise the property as soon as possible after receiving or giving notice to minimise void periods. Ideally, start advertising no sooner than one month before the property's available date.

2. Open communication is key to ensuring a smooth move-out process for both parties. Send your tenant a letter or email detailing the move-out process and reminding them of their responsibilities.

3. Schedule a meeting with your tenant at the property on the move-out date. Conduct a thorough inspection, take meter readings, and obtain a forwarding address for the tenant. Compare the property's current condition with the initial inventory to identify any discrepancies or issues that need to be addressed.

4. The deposit should be refunded to the tenant once you are satisfied that the property is in acceptable condition. If there are any disputes regarding the property's condition, allow the tenant an opportunity to rectify the problem.

5. In cases where an agreement cannot be reached between the landlord and tenant, the Alternative Dispute Resolution Service may be used. It is crucial to never commit to releasing the deposit on the move-out day and to advise any possible deductions within five days of the tenancy's end.

Conclusion

A. REFLECTION AND FUTURE UPDATES

This book was crafted to serve as a concise yet informative guide for landlords, covering various aspects of property management. While it touches upon many critical points, there is an extensive amount of detail that could be explored further in each area. As regulations and best practices evolve, this book will be updated and expanded to remain relevant and helpful.

B. STAYING INFORMED AND UPDATED

As a token of gratitude for your purchase, I will provide you with a PDF update for each new revision of this book. To receive these updates, simply send your details via email to rob.bryer@thegood.co.uk. Your feedback, comments, and suggestions are invaluable for enhancing this guide, so please do not hesitate to get in touch.

C. SEEKING ADDITIONAL ADVICE AND SUPPORT

If you ever need further advice or assistance, feel

free to email me, call my office at 01303 647221, or visit our website to find your local Good Estate Agent. Our team of experienced professionals at TheGoodEstateAgent.com is dedicated to helping landlords navigate the challenges and complexities of property management.

D. A RECAP OF KEY POINTS

Throughout this guide, we have explored essential topics that every landlord should be aware of, including:

The responsibilities and expectations of being a landlord
Finding and selecting the right tenant
Preparing the property for rent
Creating a comprehensive inventory
Drafting a legally compliant tenancy agreement
Ensuring the property meets safety regulations and standards
Managing rent and deposits
Facilitating a smooth move-in process
Conducting regular inspections and addressing concerns
Navigating the move-out process and ending the tenancy on a positive note
By understanding and implementing the strategies and advice shared in this guide, you can create a

successful and positive experience for both you and your tenants.

E. MOVING FORWARD WITH CONFIDENCE

Property management can be a rewarding and lucrative endeavor when approached with the right mindset and armed with the proper knowledge. This guide aims to provide you with the foundational understanding necessary to navigate the world of property management with confidence. As you continue to learn and grow in your role as a landlord, remember to seek guidance, stay informed, and adapt to the ever-changing landscape of the rental market.

Embrace the journey ahead and take pride in your role as a successful and responsible landlord, contributing to a better and more enjoyable rental experience for all parties involved.

Gillion

Me 07729, 087 252

CF82 78F

17   H

12 Thursday

c

Printed in Great Britain
by Amazon

24143458R00066